This book is dedicated to all who find Nature

not an adversary to conquer and destroy, but a storehouse

of infinite knowledge and experience linking man to

all things past and present. They know conserving the natural

environment is essential to our future well-being.

WildLife @ YELLOWSTONE

THE STORY BEHIND THE SCENERY®

by Sue Consolo-Murphy and Kerry Murphy

Sue Consolo-Murphy and Kerry Murphy met in Yellowstone, where both work for the National Park Service. Sue is a resource naturalist and writer-editor of park publications. Kerry earned a Ph.D. studying mountain lions and now works as a wildlife biologist with the wolf project.

Yellowstone National Park, *located in the northwestern corner of Wyoming, is the world's first national park. Established in 1872, it conserves unique geologic features, scenery, and wildlife.*

Front cover: Bull elk bugling, photo by Jeff Foott. Inside front cover: Gray wolf mother nuzzles her pup, photo by Alan and Sandy Carey. Page 1: Clark's nutcracker, photo by Neal and Mary Jane Mishler. Page 2/3: Bison herd in Lamar Valley, photo by Thomas D. Mangelsen.

Edited by Cheri C. Madison. Book design by K. C. DenDooven.

First Printing, 1999

LC 99-60067. ISBN 0-88714-149-8.

"We...came to a beautiful flat, which we gave the name of Buffalo Flat, as we found thousands of buffalo quietly grazing... this flat...with numerous lakes scattered over it and the

THOMAS D. MANGELSEN

finest range in the world. Here we found all manner of wild game—
buffalo, elk, blacktail deer, bear, and moose."

-A. Bart Henderson, prospector, 1870

The Pyramid of Life

WildLife @ Yellowstone

Life in Balance

Wild residents of Yellowstone coexist in a long-term balance, one that is greatly influenced by natural processes—drought, fire, flooding, and winter weather. The park provides a stunning backdrop in which to observe animals throughout the changing seasons.

Spring is a time for birth of many animals, and the return of migrant birds. Snow gives way to rain showers. Rivers fill with runoff. Plants "green up," providing lush growth for grazing animals to eat. Predators seek food by hunting newborn grazers.

Summer means long, hot days and little rainfall. Plants dry out, losing much of their food value. Wildlife move progressively higher to seek green plants near the mountaintops.

In autumn, animals replace lighter fur with thicker winter coats. Birds head south. Elk, deer, and moose perform ritualized mating displays. Hibernators go underground as snow piles up. Predators and scavengers have a bounty of food available as winter takes its toll on vulnerable prey.

Even as spring reappears, many wildlife subjected to the ravages of brutal cold, deep snow, and scarce food succumb to "winterkill." Nothing goes to waste. An animal dies—others consume it to survive, eventually recycling minerals into the soil, stimulating new plant growth—and the cycle continues.

GERALD & BUFF CORSI

Elk calves, born in May or June are often seen in the valleys of the park's major rivers. Newborns struggle to their feet in the first day or two of life. Their spotted coloring helps camouflage them from predators. They are especially vulnerable until they reach a month old. Calves stay close to their mothers, nursing and eating grasses within a few weeks.

GEORGE ROBBINS

A coyote pulls meat from the remains of an elk which died the previous night. First-year elk calves and mature bulls, weakened by energy expended during rutting activities in the fall, are especially subject to winter When carcasses are scarce, scavengers can pick a large animal clean to the bone within 24 hours of its death. At other times, when carrion is plentiful, animals like coy and eagles select only the choicest portions to eat. Bones are left for rodents to gnaw on; hide, hooves, and cartilage remain for maggots and carrion beetles to decompose.

The most abundant large mammal in Yellowstone, about 30,000 elk in eight major herds spend summers in the park. About half of those are year-round, or resident, herds found in northern Yellowstone, and along the Firehole and Madison river valleys warmed by runoff from geysers and hot springs. A mature cow elk weighs 350 to 500 pounds and can live to be 15 or more years old.

In winter, elk struggle to find food. They seek out windblown slopes, with thermally heated soil, and paw the ground to reach grasses, or browse shrubs and trees above the snowpack.

GLENN VAN NIMWEGEN

Elk move throughout summer, seeking succulent grasses first along river bottoms, then under the forest canopy and, later, in high mountain meadows. Cows and calves group together. Bulls live alone or in small bands, except during autumn mating season. Elk migrate to lower elevations to spend winter months.

*Yellowstone offers visitors a rare opportunity
to observe animals interacting in a natural setting,
much as John Colter might have seen when he left
the Lewis and Clark expedition to explore the region.
Here nature reigns. The views are unpredictable,
sometimes brutal, but always fascinating, and always wild.*

Yellowstone is home to a vast array of native animals—at least 60 mammals, 12 fishes, 300 birds, 100 butterflies, and 10 reptiles and amphibians—all here when the park was established in 1872. The remarkable scenery and geology is not only lovely to behold—it provides wildlife the food and shelter they need to live.

The rocks and soils, foundation of the landscape, support more than 1,100 species of plants. Animals that eat plants are called grazers or herbivores, the most abundant and visible of Yellowstone's wildlife. Scavengers and decomposers absorb nutrients from the carcasses of dead animals and eventually return them to the soil. Meat-eating predators, despite their fierce reputations, depend mostly on grazers for survival and are less abundant in both species and numbers—and thus are seen less often by visitors. Scientists decry the common maxim that predators control their prey, or argue that the opposite may be true.

Predator populations are linked to the numbers (prey, but factors such as weather and cover influence how predators and their prey are able t coexist. In Yellowstone, where wildlife habitat ha been protected from human development, it is th predators that are endangered species—wolve grizzlies, bald eagles, and peregrine falcons.

While some animals can be classified as stric ly herbivore or carnivore, others are less particula about their diets. Many predators which kill to ea also scavenge meat killed by others. Bears are om nivores which use all three feeding strategies a various times. Together, plants and animals mak up different communities which, collectively, eco ogists say make up a pyramid of life.

Grazers, predators, and scavengers are foun in all habitats. Some species are closely associate with a particular habitat, while others use th landscape in a less discriminating manne Yellowstone can generally be categorized as eithe forest or grassland, interspersed with rocky brea and stretching to subalpine zones above tree lin Rivers, often warmed by thermal features whic dot the park, run wild and undammed throug the ecosystem. The riparian zones along wate ways provide vital oases for many wildlife.

On any given day, the park may appear trar quil, even lacking in wild animals to be seen. The suddenly, the peaceful setting is punctuated b seemingly violent interludes. A bird swoops dow and plucks a fish from the water. A coyot pounces on a mouse. An elk calf cries for mothe as a mountain lion stalks the herd. A bison dies a winter's end, and ravens immediately pick at it scruffy remains.

The death of one living thing gives suste nance to another, and the community of lif thrives.

JOHN P. GEORGE

At birth in April or May, bison calves have a reddish coat. It is replaced by late summer with a dark brown one, a color the bison will wear for the rest of its life.

At the end of the nineteenth century, bison which once roamed the Plains and mountainous West by the millions had been nearly eliminated. Only several dozen remained, protected in the young Yellowstone National Park. Today, the park preserves a unique free-ranging herd of bison, also known as buffalo.

Bison
Bison bison

- Bison are the largest animal living in Yellowstone.
- Males (bulls) can weigh more than 2,000 pounds.
- Females (cows) are smaller, but still powerful.
- Both sexes have horns, which are not shed annually but are covered by a hard sheath.
- Bulls may be distinguished by their broader heads and horns that are thicker, with more curvature than those of females.
- Like elk, bison typically segregate into large cow-calf groups, while bulls stay to themselves.
- In July and August, bison come together for mating season, a noisy spectacle characterized by grunts and snorts from the massed herd.
- Bison mature at about age 3, and an old bison may live more than 20 years.

Bison are grazers, preferring grasses and sedges that grow in the wet meadows across the park. They are seen most often in the Hayden, Lamar, and Firehole valleys, but do spend time in the forests. Little impedes their movement—they can wade or swim the largest rivers and may be found in rocky terrain.

Despite their apparent similarity to domestic cattle, Yellowstone's bison are anything but tame. They are surprisingly fast—sprinting up to 30 miles per hour—and may be aggressive, using their horns to defend themselves or their young. Dozens of park visitors have been injured when approaching bison too closely; a few people have been seriously wounded or killed when gored by a bison. They may be safely watched from a distance or by visitors who remain in their vehicles.

Size cannot protect bison from the ultimate killer in Yellowstone—winter. Climate, more than disease or predators, controls the number of bison in the park. When they die, bison make a substantial meal for decomposers and scavengers, from tiny insects to Yellowstone's grizzly bears.

Grassland Communities

The grasslands make up less than 20 percent of Yellowstone's landscape, but are proportionately more valuable habitat for many of the wildlife species that live here. Across the northern third of the park, the Lamar and Yellowstone rivers bisect the heart of the Northern Range, home to all the hoofed species including the largest herd of elk. In the southern, heavily forested two-thirds of the park, the grasslands of the Hayden and Pelican valleys provide rare and welcome breaks in the landscape. Even above the tree line, open meadows abound with grazing animals throughout the short but precious growing season.

The abundant food plants in the grasslands support large concentrations of bison and elk. Small mammals, birds, and insects seek diversity of food and shelter among the flowers, grasses, trees, and shrubby plants. Predators, many of whom seek cover by day, home in on prey using darkness as a shield. Thus, the crepuscular hours near dusk and dawn make the best time for wildlife watching in the bustling grassland communities.

GLENN VAN NIMWEGEN

Pioneers crossing the Great Plains called them "picket pins," for their resemblance to a horseman's picket stake. The Uinta ground squirrel is often mistaken for another common grassland rodent, the prairie dog, which is not found in Yellowstone National Park. Ground squirrels live in burrows, where they hibernate for up to seven months of the year. Their underground homes also provide safe haven from hawks, badgers, weasels, and other predators. Active during daylight hours in spring and summer, they mostly nibble grasses but occasionally prey upon insects or scavenge meat from carcasses.

*I*n winter, bison swing their massive heads from side to side to clear snow up to four feet deep and reach food plants. Their heavy coats help them tolerate cold temperatures, although some bison die each year from the combined effects of poor body condition, reduced food availability, and climatic stress. Though subject to disease and parasites, these factors are not significant causes of bison mortality. Neither is predation, which has seldom been documented—except for a few cases attributed to Yellowstone's newly restored wolves.

*B*ison often travel single file, making distinct trails through the grasslands or forests. On Mary Mountain or the Mirror Plateau, Native Americans of the past and hikers of today follow bison pathways through the dense deadfall on the forest floor to reemerge in a grassy expanse suitable for camping or enjoying the view.

Although feeding and trampling on grasses appear to be destructive forces, native plants have adapted strategies that take advantage of grazing pressure. For some of Yellowstone's common grass species, grazing actually stimulates production. Nutrient cycling occurs at a high rate on heavily grazed sites, as elk and bison transfer nitrogen and phosphorus, minerals necessary for plant growth, to the soil.

11

ART WOLFE

TOM MURPHY

Bohemian waxwings winter in Yellowstone, where they are commonly seen at low elevations. Both males and females bear a black mask and distinctive crest. Though a tree-dwelling bird, they prefer open woodlands that are less dense than the park forests. Flocks are often seen speeding gracefully along the edges of the grasslands, perching to eat berries from junipers.

A young mule deer fawn peers cautiously from the security of a young pine grove, where it hides from danger such as cougars. Although they range from the foothills to the forests in summer, most of Yellowstone's mule deer migrate to northern Yellowstone and spend winter months in the sagebrush-grassland. More than elk and bison, mule deer—named for their large ears—browse shrubs and woody plants for forage.

KENT & DONNA DANNEN

Pocket gophers use their feet and large incisors to dig burrows and gnaw on food plants. In winter, they tunnel in the snow above the frozen ground, filling their shelters with old nest materials and waste matter, leaving earthen cores visible when snow melts.

Several hundred bighorn sheep live in Yellowstone, grazing high mountain meadows in summer. Intrepid hikers may see them near the summits of Mount Washburn, Mount Sheridan, Mount Holmes, or Avalanche Peak. In winter, they move to grasslands at lower elevations, and are easily spotted along the cliffs of the Gardner River Canyon. Females (ewes) congregate in bands with their lambs, joining the males (rams) during the rutting season in November and December. Mature males engage in clashing displays of ramming their massive horns, fighting for dominance and breeding opportunities. One or two lambs are born to each mother the following May or June.
Sheep escape to steep terrain when chased by eagles and coyotes, which are thought to be responsible for high lamb mortality in the park.

Grasslands in Yellowstone

The Hayden Valley, in the center of the park between Yellowstone Lake and the Grand Canyon of the Yellowstone, is a good spot to observe interactions among grassland residents, especially in summer. Try visiting in the wee hours around dawn or dusk—many animals are least active and visible during the heat of a summer day. In northeastern Yellowstone, the Lamar Valley hosts similar wildlife and plant species, and is accessible by automobile all year round. In both valleys, wildlife can be viewed safely from the many roadside pullouts without disturbing animals.

The smaller but lovely Pelican Valley is off limits to visitors in spring, the most critical season for bears, especially females with young. It may be reached on foot or horseback in summer and fall during daylight hours only.

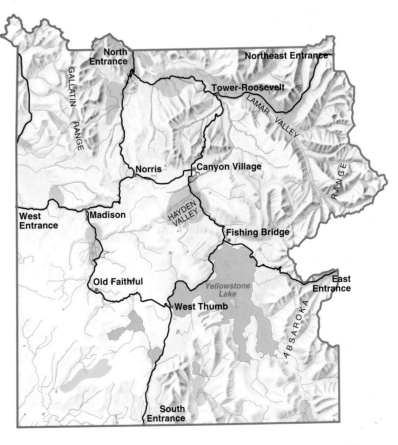

Grassland Communities

***P**ronghorn, often called antelope, are the fastest* mammal in North America. Reported as numerous in the grasslands by early Yellowstone explorers, the small and genetically isolated nature of the park's herd now concerns scientists.

The smallest of *Yellowstone's ungulates, pronghorn seldom exceed 140 pounds. They are easily recognized by their tan coats, white rumps, and black jaw patches. Both males and females have horns which, similar to antlered animals, are shed each year, usually in November. Males (bucks) are territorial and may mate with more than one female in September and October. Twin fawns are common, born in May or June in the sagebrush grasslands near Gardiner, Montana, as well as on Blacktail Deer Plateau and in the Lamar Valley. Though historically seen in the interior park valleys, they are now seldom observed in the Hayden or Firehole River valleys.*

The pronghorn herd's *decline in the park may relate to loss of winter range in lowlands outside the park, and to intense predation of fawns by coyotes, bobcats, eagles, and more recently, wolves. Young fawns are most vulnerable when bedded. On their feet, they graze close to their mothers, eating grasses, forbs, and shrubs like sagebrush. They rely on their speed to outrun danger.*

TOM MURPHY

***A**t least seven species of blue* butterflies in the genus Plebejus have been found in Yellowstone. Look for them in meadows, lighting on grasses, violets, and willows. Butterflies—which may only be collected by permitted researchers— are valued not only for their beauty, but as sensitive indicators of climate change and environmental effects of pesticides.

KENT & DONNA DANNEN

***T**he mostly overlooked deer* mice are abundant throughout the park, preferring dry habitats. These omnivores build grassy nests under rocks or logs. They eat seeds, green shoots, nuts, carrion, and insects. Active year-round, they generally live to be only a few years old.

PHOTOS BY TOM MURPHY

Gray wolves, also known as Northern Rocky Mountain wolves, conjure up differing images in the minds of humans—vicious competitor, unwanted pest, persecuted predator, endangered symbol. While similar in looks and behavior to the more common coyote, wolves are two to four times larger. Adult females weigh 90 to 100 pounds and males 120 or more pounds, standing tall above the sagebrush. Color ranges from grayish white to black, compared to their often reddish-tinted cousin. Ears and noses of wolves are less prominent on their massive heads.

RICHARD DAY

Coyotes, also subject to predator control programs that historically limited wolves, persevered because of their adaptable nature and ability to survive on smaller prey. Voles— short-tailed vegetarian rodents (pictured)—mice, and ground squirrels make up the majority of their annual diet, although they are capable of killing foxes, deer, and even full-grown elk.

From a rocky perch, a bobcat looks *for small grassland animals as prey. Reddish or yellowish-brown with black-tipped hairs and tufts at their ear tips, bobcats rarely display their presence to park visitors.*

Striped skunks are seldom seen, *but their tell-tale smell betrays their presence. At night, they search for insects, bird eggs, or carrion to eat. Their tracks may be found along streams in the northern part of the park.*

Predominantly *plant-eaters, brown-headed cowbirds perch on the back of a bison bull looking for food. Like many songbirds, they are also insect predators. In summer, bison often wallow on the ground. Kicking up dust or mud may lessen the annoyance caused by biting flies and other insects.*

Wolf Recovery Program

Early in the twentieth century, large predators were commonly viewed as destructive elements in nature, detrimental to healthy populations of popular wildlife like deer and elk. Control programs severely reduced or eliminated predator populations in much of the West, even in national parks like Yellowstone, where wolves were eliminated by the 1930s. For six decades, this native carnivore was missing, causing changes in the wildlife community.

Through studies in Yellowstone and other wild lands, biologists such as Adolph Murie and Aldo Leopold paved the way in rethinking the importance of predators in influencing animal and plant communities. In 1995, after years of evolution in environmental thinking and intense public debate, wolves were returned to Yellowstone, brought from Canada as part of a plan to help this endangered species. Once again, wolves are part of the Yellowstone panorama.

The goal of wolf restoration is to establish a healthy population—10 breeding pairs—in and around the park, and also in northwestern Montana and central Idaho, where ample prey and habitat exist. Relatively low-density human populations make for less wildlife-human conflicts. Special rules were enacted to ensure that, outside parks, wolves that threaten domestic livestock could be controlled. Fortunately, in the first years of the recovery program, most wolves have stayed within Yellowstone Park and adjacent wilderness areas, eating wild animals. Elk, moose, and deer are favored prey, although wolves have also killed bison, beaver, and pronghorn. By 1998, more than 100 wolves roamed the greater Yellowstone ecosystem, thrilling thousands of park visitors lucky enough to find their tracks, hear their howls, or see them running free.

Biologists with the U.S. Fish and Wildlife Service journeyed to Alberta and British Columbia, Canada, in 1995 and 1996 to capture and bring 31 wolves from areas with similar terrain and food species to Yellowstone. Data on wolves' ages, sex, pelt color, weight, body condition and blood were collected prior to transport. Each wolf also received a radio collar to help track its movements after being released into the wild. The animals released ranged from 72 to 120 pounds, and varied from near-white to black. Family groups or paired animals were held for about ten weeks in specially built acclimation pens and fed road-killed bison, elk, and deer during their temporary captivity designed to discourage the wolves from bolting back to Canada. The technique worked—some founder wolves even bred in the pens, producing unexpected litters of pups in the first two years of restoration.

Like other wild canids,
wolves are social animals.
Most live in packs, led by a dominant, or alpha, male and female. Mating season is in February or March;
pups are born in April or May at dens dug into the ground or hidden among rocks or fallen trees. Non-breeding
pack members help feed young wolves, and as soon as they are capable, pups begin learning to kill the
food they need to survive. By their second year, subadults begin to disperse from the pack, seeking their own
mates. Wolves vigorously defend their territory from other wolf packs that venture too close. A long-lived
wolf reaches the age of ten or more years in the wild.

Yellowstone offers an
unparalleled opportunity to
research the effects of wolves
on the wildlife community. In
the years prior to and since the
wolves' return, scientists
have amassed data on prey
populations as well as potential
competitors. Students compete
for the chance to participate in
documenting wolf movements, denning
behavior, reproductive success,
predation, and interactions with other
bird and animal species.

Researchers use modern technology,
such as radio transmitters, to track
wolf packs and determine the success
of the restoration effort. Sometimes
simple observation—easily achieved
on wolves visible in the park's open
grasslands—is the biologist's best method,
accomplished with persistence even
during the coldest days of winter.

*F*ierce nocturnal grassland predators, badgers use their long claws to excavate pocket gophers, field mice, and ground squirrels from their burrows. They also dig sizable holes to use as temporary cover while hunting—or being hunted by larger predators such as wolves.

TOM & PAT LEESON

ERWIN & PEGGY BAUER

GARY LEPPART

*C*oyotes and badgers often compete for prey. The two are sometimes seen traveling together in apparent efforts to take advantage of each other's missed opportunities. In this encounter, the canid looks to have won the small mamma morsel. On another occasion, a rodent who escapes a pouncing coyote may flee towa a burrow, only to find a waiting badger. All's fair in a day's work for each animal, doing whatever it takes to survive.

*T*he park's high altitude and cold environme make it inhospitable for most snakes. Two garte snake species are found, and prairie rattlesnake den at the lowest elevations. The bull snake (pictured) is also called a gopher snake, after on of its common prey. It squeezes its victims to de

GLENN VAN NIMWEGEN

***C**liff swallows nest in large* colonies, constructing mud nests on steep-sided rock faces. The birds prey on insects such as dragonflies, spiders, beetles, and—to our appreciation—mosquitoes. Although associated with the sagebrush grasslands of the park, cliff swallows may also be seen along the Yellowstone River in the Grand Canyon. Several other swallow species summer in Yellowstone, including bank swallows, tree swallows, and violet-green swallows, which are often seen near ponds and riverbanks in the geyser basins of the Firehole River valley.

GLENN VAN NIMWEGEN

***T**he brilliance of the mountain* bluebird stands out against the starkness of an old cliff swallow colony, where it feeds its young. Bluebirds signal the arrival of spring in Yellowstone, returning as early as March, and nesting in late May and early June. They often hover above the grassland and catch an insect in flight. Or they light on a sagebrush bush before dropping to the ground to feed on ants, caterpillars, grasshoppers, or beetles. Come autumn, mountain bluebirds migrate to the Southwest or cross the border to Mexico.

W. PERRY CONWAY

High above the grassland, golden eagles may be seen soaring in summer or winter. Adults are easily distinguished from the slightly smaller bald eagle by their uniform brown appearance, though the golden tint of their head and neck is apparent at close range. In Yellowstone, golden eagles nest atop cliffs overlook wide open valleys where prey is abundant. Ground squirrels, snakes, and mice are easily caught in the eagle's sharp talon Occasionally, golden eagles kill larger animals, such as pronghorn, and they scavenge carrion when available.

Eagle nests may be several feet in diameter, built of sticks and brush. Typica two eaglets are born to an eagle pair in May or June. The young do not learn to f for two or more months, relying on their parents to bring food back to the nest.

JEFFREY RICH

Heard as often as it is seen, a western meadowlark sings its flute-like song while perched on a dried plant stalk. Studies show that meadowlarks eat some grains and seeds, but the majority of their diet is animal matter— beetles, caterpillars, crane flies, snails, and spiders. These birds may be sighted in the Lamar Valley in summer, but leave Yellowstone for warmer winter climates. The meadowlark is the state bird of both Montana and Wyoming.

JEFF VANUGA

Hundreds of sandhill cranes live here from April through September, their unique, rattling call echoing across the meadows. Up to four feet tall, the birds are occasionally mistaken for deer! Cranes perform elaborate mating dances, leaping and bowing their necks as they circle their mates. They build grassy nests on the ground in wet meadows or near ponds, eating amphibians, crayfish, insects, small mammals, and plants. Sensitive to disturbance, a crane will harass or lead intruders away from nesting areas. Researchers have watched grizzly bears chase sandhills for food or sport. No bears were successful.

In brushy thickets and willows found along the waterways, yellow warblers hunt for larvae, moths, and other insects to feed their young. Brown-headed cowbirds often lay their own eggs in warbler nests, where the host birds unsuspectingly feed the invader. This is an example of nest parasitism, benefiting the cowbird but not the warbler.

JEFF FOOTT

TOM M

Alert for disturbance, a sow grizzly bear and her three cubs scavenge meat from a bison. She rises up on her hind legs to improve her view. Although capable of killing large animals, bears do not waste energy hunting when meat is readily availab Grizzlies range across the park in all habitats, but are most visible in the grasslands during spring and early summer, when winterkill and young elk calves provide valuable protein for the hungry bruins. Thoug bears will often seek cover in the forest or under darkness of night, they once ranged across the Great Pla relying more on their size and strength to protect them from danger—which comes mostly from humans.

The ubiquitous black-billed magpies, easily recognized by their nearly foot-long tails and black and white coloring, pick at a carcass. Members of the crow family, magpies caught the notice of Lewis and Clark when raiding the explorers' camp for food. Magpies build bulky twig nests in low-lying thickets. Nests are often reused by owls, small hawks, robins, or other songbirds. Like other scavengers, the birds play an important if unglamorous role in cleaning up the remains of dead animals

ALAN & SANDY CAREY

Little remains of a bison carcass being inspected by a coyote and a magpie. In time, even the bison's vertebrae and skull will decay, assisted by decomposers or "detritivores," such as carrion beetles. Beetles consume everything from live and dead wood to animal dung, and make up the largest order of life on Earth. One researcher found 57 species of beetles strongly associated with carcasses, feeding either directly on the meat or on other insects. New grass, reaping the benefit of nutrients recycled from such winterkill, appears greener and taller than the surrounding plants. This ultimately feeds other grazers and predators.

KENT & DONNA DANNEN

Chipmunks gnaw on an antler shed by a mule deer buck in midwinter. Beginning each spring, male elk, moose, and deer that are in good condition regrow their antlers, fed by blood vessels in the velvety growth on the outside of the bone. By late summer, antler growth ceases. The blood vessels dry up, and the animals begin to shed their velvet by scraping it against trees. By the onset of each ungulate's rutting season, the antlers are clean of the velvet sheath and become weapons used in sparring matches between males. Removing antlers from the park is prohibited; even the bony growth is used by other members of the wildlife community. Rodents obtain needed minerals from the decaying antlers.

25

Forest Communities

About 80 percent of Yellowstone is covered by forests. Yet surprisingly few distinct species make up the tree-covered landscape. The vast majority of trees are lodgepole pines, known here for their straight trunks, around which Native Americans used to center their tipis. These lodgepole forests are closely associated with unproductive soils that overlay the deposits from the Yellowstone caldera, site of massive volcanic activity between 2 million and 600,000 years ago. Subalpine fir, Engelmann spruce, and whitebark pine are conifers that grow at high elevations in soils formed from volcanic deposits that are about 50 million years old. Limber pine and Douglas fir are found at low elevations of the park. Several species of juniper are found, both in tree and shrub form. Deciduous trees—such as aspen, cottonwood, and alder—which lose their leaves in winter are sparse indeed.

Beneath the forest overstory lie grasses, flowers, mosses, lichens, and other herbaceous plants known as forbs. For the park's large acreage, it has relatively low vegetative diversity—which affects the variety of animals that live in the forests. Still, a walk in the woods can yield fascinating wildlife sightings to those who are patient and alert.

*A **grizzly bear cub swats at a bee**, reminding us that size alone does not make animals immune to annoyance or distraction from their fellow creatures. Bear cubs, both grizzlies and the smaller black bears which also live in greater Yellowstone, are born in January or February inside a den dug into a hillside or under exposed tree roots. Blind and hairless at birth, young grizzlies remain with their mothers for two more winters, while black bear cubs usually stay only one winter after emerging from their dens in April or May. Bears give birth to between one and four cubs, but litters of two are most common. While mother bear's lessons help her young learn to survive, male bears take no part in rearing their young.*

ERWIN & PEGGY BAUER

Imagine eating for only seven or eight months to survive all year. "To him almost every thing is food except granite," wrote John Muir in 1901. Grizzly bears can out-sprint the fastest human despite their bulk, which insulates them through the long, cold winters.

Grizzly Bear
Ursus arctos

- Females (sows) weigh about 250 to 350 pounds.
- Males (boars) may weigh up to 800 pounds.
- Males and females socialize only when mating in May and June.
- Mothers tend cubs alone, and subadult siblings may remain together just after leaving her care at about age three.
- Grizzlies mature at age five or six, and in Yellowstone have lived as long as 28 years.

Grizzlies graze on roots, flowers, and berries. They prey upon rodents, fish, elk calves, even full-grown moose—and scavenge carrion and steal kills from mountain lions or wolves. They eat moths that burrow among talus slopes, and steal nuts cached by squirrels. Then from about November through March, they sleep. Only the long claws and mass of adult grizzlies prevent them from climbing trees, as black bears do.

Bears and Yellowstone are synonymous to the American public. But hunting outside the park and management actions within, taken to ensure the safety of visitors, resulted in the grizzly bears' decline. In 1975, they were given protection under the Endangered Species Act. In the last decade of the twentieth century, the population increased and expanded well beyond Yellowstone Park.

The greatest threat to their survival is the loss of habitat to human encroachment. Guns, vehicles, and wildlife managers, forced to remove bears that conflict with livestock or humans, also kill bears. Cubs may be killed by other large predators, but a full-grown grizzly bear fears little in the wildlife community.

A black bear nibbles buffalo berries and currants. Though bears eat raspberries, strawberries, and huckleberries, the park is too dry to support good crops of these and other fruits, which make up a small part of Yellowstone bears' diets. The name black bear is misleading—they may be black, any shade of brown, and (rarely) even near-white in color. Black bears are found more often in forests than grizzly bears, a separation that benefits black bears by keeping them out of the way of the larger, more aggressive grizzlies. Wise hikers keep company and make noise to warn bears of their presence. Most often, bears scurry away before they are seen or encountered by visitors.

JEFF FOOTT

One of Yellowstone's most common year-round residents, the Clark's nutcracker, may have jammed the cone into the stump, making it easier to remove the seeds upon which the bird feeds. This noisy bird plays an important role in the reproduction and survival of a number of other species. Though sometimes an insect-eater or meat-scavenger, the nutcracker is most deservedly known for prying seeds from the cones of limber and whitebark pines. Thousands of seeds may be cached, used later by the nutcracker, or stolen by a red squirrel, a bear, or a fellow bird in the forest. Seeds that escape being eaten may sprout new pine trees.

28

A red squirrel cuts cones from a spruce to extract favored winter food. Timing of cone removal is crucial—it must be done before cones open and seeds blow away. Whitebark pines are particularly valued due to the large size and high fat content of the seeds.

Cones are stored in middens up to 25 feet across and several feet deep, used repeatedly for years. Squirrels' caches, like the nutcrackers', benefit other birds and mammals. Bears are efficient at raiding middens, scraping scales off the cones, and eating seeds in late summer and autumn.

Chattering red squirrels actively defend their territories from others. Females tolerate males for just one day of breeding. Three to five young are born a month later, and she raises them alone. Within a year, they must move to their own territory, where they chance becoming prey of a hungry hawk.

Forested Areas of Yellowstone

Finding forested areas of the park is easy—finding wildlife in them may take a bit more effort. Around most of the Grand Loop Road, the massive figure eight that winds through the heart of the park, you will find lodgepole pine forests. Any number of trails into the woods will offer opportunities to see small mammals, birds, and perhaps even a large predator lurking among the trees. At higher elevations near Dunraven and Sylvan passes, and in the northeastern corner of the park, spruce-fir forests line park roads. Here the cover is more dense and the undergrowth thicker, and the wildlife watching offers different rewards. Deciduous forests are most uncommon in the park, though aspen groves may be seen near the Gallatin Highway along the park's northwestern edge, along Blacktail Plateau Drive, and in the Lamar Valley.

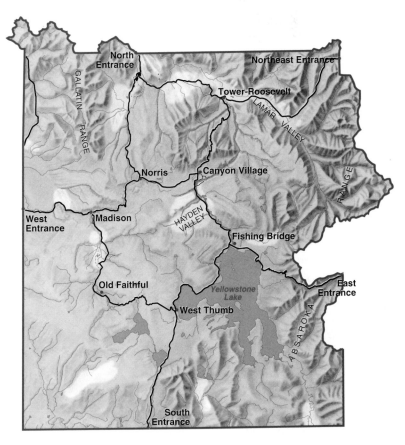

JACKIE GILMORE

***Y**ellow-bellied* marmots, a western groundhog, are herbivorous rodents that excavate tunnels or live in rock piles. Their hibernation may last from September through April, although they sometimes emerge from burrows before winter's end. They mate soon after, and live in colonies. Near Old Faithful, hairless marmots have often exited dens. Tests ruled out diseases and mineral imbalance, causing speculation that they shed unneeded hair in their thermally heated homes. Also known as rockchucks, or whistle pigs for their sharp call, marmots are pursued by hunters such as eagles, coyotes, bears, and young cougars.

***B**road-tailed* hummingbirds nest in the forests, feeding on nectar as well as an occasional insect they find among the flowers. Like the calliope hummingbird which also summers in Yellowstone, these tiny birds migrate south of the border for winter, prompting Yellowstone and Mexican biologists to establish cooperative programs to monitor such species' welfare.

JEFF VANUGA

***A** young porcupine and its mother show off their sha*[r]p quills. These famed defensive tools are modified hairs, which don't deter predators such as cougars. Porcupines [are] good climbers, eating mostly conifer needles and bark, sometimes girdling trees. They also eat leaves, roots, and other vegetation on the ground, and may be seen waddling along park roadways at night.

JEFF VANUGA

During most of the season, mule deer appear tranquil, browsing among the forest shrubs and forbs. But during the autumn rut, bucks vie for breeding opportunities. They are polygamous, and can be quite aggressive as they rub velvet from their antlers and use them in fighting for females. Males have multi-forked antlers while white-tailed deer, who are uncommon here, have tines that branch from one primary beam. In the fall, most deer migrate outside the park, where they may be legally hunted. Predators, such as wolves and cougars, and winter also limit a deer's life-span.

MICHAEL H. FRANCIS

A tiny pika, also called a coney or rock rabbit, scampers among a talus slope, where hawks and pine martens hunt for them. In Yellowstone, they are most often found at higher elevations. Listen for their high-pitched call, then closely watch a rock pile for this hamster-size creature. Pikas forage all summer on grasses, lichens, leaves, and twigs. They store them in "haystacks" beneath the rocks, and rely on the stored food all winter, instead of hibernating. Pikas may have several litters of young each year.

Overleaf: A gray wolf pushes through snow on the trail of prey. Wolf packs make kills on the average of every two to five days, their movements undeterred even in the mountains on Yellowstone's borders. Photo by Erwin and Peggy Bauer.

31

GLENN VAN NIMWEGEN

JEFF VANUGA

A female hairy woodpecker feeds on a moth. The birds may find food by feeling or listening for insects while perched on the trunk of a tree.

Swooping low, a great gray owl hunts for prey in a marshy meadow near the coniferous forest.

One bird that cannot be overlooked is the common raven, here resting on the edge of the Grand Canyon of the Yellowstone River. The largest of all perching birds, in flight it may at first glance be mistaken for an eagle. An omnivore, the raven may prey upon frogs and bird eggs, or graze fall berries. Mostly, it scavenges. Ravens actively follow bears, canids, and ungulate herds, waiting for opportunities to feed on carrion.

ED COOPER

In a quest to colle
wildlife sightings
photographs, son
visitors miss th
mystery and beau
of animal sign.
story, unobserved,
written in the sno
we can only wono
when and wh
encounter mig
have taken plac
An hour, o
night ago, a sm
creature, perha
a tiny squirr
bounded across
opening. Wa:
a hawk or a rav
that pounc
unexpectedly, leav
wing and tail pri
on the untrodc
expanse of white?
we feel for b
predator and pre

The lynx and the hare are linked in biology and lore, but are lynx in Yellowstone? More numerous in boreal forests farther north, early park explorers reported occasionally trapping the small cat. Yet barely 60 lynx sightings have been recorded in the park's history. In 1998, the U.S. Fish and Wildlife Service moved to add this predator to the endangered species list. Their large, furred paws help them bound across the frozen landscape in pursuit of snowshoe hares and other small prey. (Photographed in captivity)

A pine marten, a member of the weasel family, rests on a tree branch. A common resident of Yellowstone's spruce-fir and lodgepole forests, martens prey primarily on mice and voles, but also may vary their diet with flying squirrels, insects, fruits, and berries. In winter, they seek cover in downed trees and coarse woody debris atop the snowpack. Males are territorial. Females, like bears, experience delayed implantation prior to giving birth to litters of one to five young in March or April. Rangers at snowbound posts such as Grant Village and Old Faithful must carefully secure garbage in winter, lest the martens invade the trash bins.

Poised to pounce, a red fox keeps close watch for small mammals such as mice and rabbits. The fox, a mostly nocturnal hunter, may cache unused food for a later meal. Despite their name, red foxes in northeastern Yellowstone often exhibit a distinct, paler coat. Biologists are studying this clever mountain fox, which may be a unique subspecies. Elsewhere in the park, foxes range from red to nearly black on their backs, but always with pointed ears and a white-tipped tail. Fox families dig a den or take over an abandoned badger hole and may use it for years. Often killed by coyotes, foxes may benefit from the restoration of wolves, which has resulted in a decline in coyotes.

ERWIN & PEGGY BAUER

Long-tailed (left) and short-tailed weasels (center, right) live in the park, with the latter found more often in the forests. They are effective predators, hunting shrews, mice, and insects, but also take prey even larger than themselves, such as rabbits. These small mammals are mustelids, animals with unusually large scent glands which produce quite an odor. Both weasels have black-tipped tails and turn white in winter, an adaptation that helps them hide in the snow from predators. It is the short-tailed weasel that is also known as the ermine, though both were valued by trappers for their winter pelts. In Yellowstone, weasels are hunted by rattlesnakes, owls, hawks, and foxes.

SANDY CAREY

TOM MURPHY

TOM MURPHY

__T__wo young wolves sleep quietly among some arrowleaf balsamroots. Pups immediately begin to learn about wolf society as they vie for access to mother's milk. They engage in playful fighting, and eat regurgitated food brought to the den by other pack members. The ability to feed, and eventually breed, depends on a wolf's place in the hierarchy of its pack.

__On the banks of the Gardner River, a black bear rests after eating a mule deer. Bears and cougars__ *sometimes bury remains of their food, lying possessively nearby to defend it from intruders. Thus, it's wise to give wide berth when finding a dead animal in the woods. At other times, predators tolerate others—the noisy magpie, or a hungry coyote—stealing in for a bite. On average, a winterkilled animal is at least half-eaten (by all scavengers) within one or two days of its death.*

__Black bears feed__ *less on carcasses than grizzlies, partly because they spend less time in areas where most elk and bison live and die. Human activity along park roads and near developments such as Old Faithful also causes bears to avoid carcasses that might otherwise provide a meal.*

The wolverine is a little studied
and rarely seen Yellowstone resident.
Scavenger and hunter, this bear-like creature has
been tracked across ungulate ranges and avalanche
paths in winter. In summer, rangers stationed at
fire lookout towers occasionally spot them wandering
high atop the Gallatin and Washburn ranges.

The keen-eyed red-tailed hawk pauses
while hunting rodents. Soaring over the
forests or the Grand Canyon, these hawks may
scream while courting or defending their nests.

A wolf bares its teeth, warning an invader disturbing his meal. Observational studies of wolves reveal
*that the animals have their own distinct body language. Facial and tail positions vary when the animals
express suspicion, threats, anxiety, restraint, or an invitation to mating or other social interactions. Wolves also
communicate by sound, using whimpers, growls, and other noises. Communication contributes to harmony
within a wolf pack, whose members understand the language and actively or passively defer to the leaders.
Visitors can interpret animals' body language. Approaching wildlife usually causes them to move off.
Push too far, and they may turn and face you, flattening their ears, stiffening their stance, or raising their
hackles. Pawing the ground,
growling, or snorting means trouble!*

Big and little brown bats use echolocation to hunt aquatic insects, flying beetles, and moths. These bats breed in autumn and hibernate in winter. In early summer, females form nursery colonies and bear young. They roost in hollow trees or caves— and some of the park's old buildings! Bats feed mostly at night and must keep alert for predators such as hawks and owls.

A female Williamson's sapsucker rests on an aspen branch eating ants, her favorite prey. These woodpeckers also drill rows of holes in the bark of lodgepole pines to find insect larvae and suck the sap from inside the tree.

Northern goshawks use stealth, their sharp talons, and the strong grip of their feet to kill grouse, tree squirrels, and other prey for their young. Females fiercely defend their nests, built in densely forested areas.

A robin chick gets a sizable insect mouthful from its parent. Other meals include worms and berries. Robins are associated with all of Yellowstone's forest types, from the lowlands to the highest elevations.

Few visitors are fortunate enough to see one of Yellowstone's resident mountain lions, or cougars. Sparsely distributed but not endangered, these efficient hunters of elk, deer, bighorn sheep, and porcupines scavenge infrequently. Wolves and bears often displace cougars from their kills, sometimes even killing them. Cougars, especially males, may kill their own kind, particularly young males that intrude on their territory. They are known to occasionally stalk and kill humans, but this has never happened in Yellowstone. Cougars seek rocky terrain for stalking prey and for security. They use large home ranges throughout the park in summer, and in winter, concentrate their wanderings in northern Yellowstone where prey is abundant. Mating usually occurs from February through May. Females alone raise two to four kittens until they disperse at about age one.

Ravens build large nests of sticks in trees or on cliffs, such as this rhyolite face in Yellowstone. Nesting occurs in early spring. The female lays four to six eggs and incubates them, though the male assists in bringing food and water to the young birds. The brood fledges by mid-July. Though a member of the same family, the raven is twice as large as the common crow. Ravens are highly adaptable and clever, and may live to be more than 20 years old.

TOM MURPHY

A *young grizzly scavenges* meat from a bison carcass as the spring landscape greens up. Although analyses of bear scats indicate that a majority of their diet is plants, recent studies reveal that meat has been underrepresented in these samples. Since grizzlies ceased relying on dumped garbage in the 1970s, they are more likely to have their first cubs at a younger age. Also, litters of three or even four cubs are now more common.

W. PERRY CONWAY

On a well-tracked snowscape, *a coyote makes off with an elk leg. Although a pack of coyotes can kill full-grown elk or deer, they typically scavenge from animals killed by other predators, vehicles, or the stresses of winter. Yellowstone's coyotes grow larger than in most other areas of the western United States, from 25 to 40 pounds. Still, living in packs of seven or more coyotes provides advantages in social and hunting opportunities. Coyotes can become conditioned to humans and roadside handouts, even approaching and biting visitors. For your own safety and for theirs, never approach or feed wildlife.*

The hunter-scavenger becomes *food for another carrion-feeder. The average life-span for a Yellowstone coyote is 6 years, though one marked animal lived to be at least 13 before she was preyed upon by a cougar. Coyotes, especially young pups, may succumb to diseases such as distemper and canine parvovirus. As adults, they are more often killed by other predators or by collisions with vehicles. Outside the park, they may be hunted or trapped. The manner of death is not important to the hungry magpie.*

A New Beginning

In 1988, wildfires swept across Yellowstone and adjacent lands in strength and numbers never seen by those alive today. Such large-scale natural events occur on a time scale much different than that of a human's life.

The world's oldest national park turned 125 in 1997; no one alive remembers its establishment. But scientists know that huge, intense fires had burned across the region in the early 1700s. They were fascinated, rather than shocked, by the crowning trees crackling in wind-driven fire storms that raged from July to September of that long, hot summer. More than a third of the park—793,880 acres—was burned. The news stories displayed pictures of blackened acres, and firefighters told tales of heroic efforts all for naught. Only the first snows of the season dampened the blazes, and smokes were still visible on the forest floor as drifts deepened in November.

When the flames died out, the scientists eagerly returned, competing for the chance to study the effects of fire on the human attitude, the region's economy, the plants, and the wildlife of the Yellowstone ecosystem. Another chapter of the story was just beginning.

Soon after the fires, hawks and great gray owls (pictured) easily captured rodents that had lost their protective ground cover. Most of the habitat loss for small mammals was short-lived, as ash left by the fires fertilized new growth.

Large animals such as elk, moose, deer, and bears usually moved out of harm's way during the fire season. In several spots, fire and smoke trapped dozens of elk; radio-collared bears and large numbers of circling birds later led biologists to discover the scavengers' bounty. In the winters following 1988, researchers noticed elk eating burned bark of lodgepole pines. While first thought to be a starvation diet, it turned out that charred trunks were more digestible and higher in crude protein than unburned trees, creating a temporary extra food source.

Cavity-nesting birds gained
nest trees, while songbirds that
rely on green foliage temporarily lost some
habitat. Trees, like individual animals,
have a limited life-span; many pines were
dead prior to the fires, killed by beetle
infestations as they passed 100 years of age.
The bright blue of the robin's eggs provides
lively contrast to the scarred forest.

The fires opened up the forest canopy,
allowing more sunlight to reach plants. They
also cleared away older trees and shrubs, increasing the rate of decomposition and
cycling nutrients into food plants for grazers. For several years post-fire, grass productivity actually increased
during summer. Although numbers of elk and bison had declined due to combined effects of the fires and
winterkill immediately following the fiery summer, both species quickly returned to pre-1988 levels. The heat
from the flames opened sealed, serotinous cones of lodgepole pines, releasing as many as a million seeds
per acre. Underneath the blackened forests, young trees burst forth in suitable sites. Windblown aspen
seeds proliferated, resulting in unforeseen numbers of seedlings that were widely distributed. Some may
survive heavy grazing pressure to grow into tall aspen trees.

Studies of fish, insects, mammals, and birds reveal that different species reacted in different ways to the
fires—some gained, some lost, in the time span observed thus far. Ecologists remind us that in the long run,
all the native plants and animals in Yellowstone evolved with fire. Historic fire suppression by humans may
have been more detrimental than were the conflagrations.

Aquatic Communities

"This great river has its source in the mountains... Its banks are well supplied with wood...The buffalo and other wild animals rove in herds along its banks..."

JEAN BAPTISTE TRUDEAU, CANADIAN EXPLORER, 1796, ON HEARING OF THE YELLOWSTONE RIVER

Woven among the grassland and forest tapestry are Yellowstone's waters, an estimated 220 lakes and 1,000 streams. Water covers about 5 percent of the park's surface area. Twelve native fishes live in the waters, and some 400 types of aquatic insects have been recorded in the park. In fact, an estimated 80 percent of Wyoming's native animals rely at times on riparian zones—landscapes along rivers and creeks. These same areas attract visitors, drawn to try a hand at fishing, watch for birds along the banks, launch a canoe across a glassy lake, or just listen to the soothing sound of water trickling over the rocks.

Yellowstone and surrounding wilderness lands are shaped by, and today protect, the headwaters of five major rivers. The park straddles the Continental Divide. The Yellowstone, Madison, and Gallatin rivers join the Missouri, then the Mississippi, terminating in the Atlantic Ocean. The Falls and Snake rivers are part of the mighty Columbia River system which flows to the Pacific. Despite early drives to harness their power, park rivers remain free-flowing. Deep, cold lakes and shallow ponds and wetlands that freeze in winter pockmark the landscape, harboring unlimited wildlife viewing opportunities at any time of year.

GLENN VAN NIMWEGEN

A *precocious river otter rests on a log with its fresh catch of the day, a cutthroat trout. An otter may range dozens of miles along the shore of a river, such as the Yellowstone or the Lamar. Otters spend much of their day denned up in bank holes, logjams, and even beaver lodges. Despite their name, otters also live in lakes. In winter, look for signs of their sliding down a steep bank or across the ice above the Upper Falls of the Yellowstone. They are often seen using holes in the ice on Yellowstone Lake near the West Thumb Geyser Basin. Coyotes and other predators may hunt otters. Bald eagles, gulls, and pelicans attempt to steal fish from this sleek animal angler.*

Watch a bald eagle soaring high above the Yellowstone River, and marvel at the bird's perspective, even envy the view it must have of the land and water below. Are eagles always on the lookout for prey?

Bald Eagle
Haliaeetus leucocephalus

ALAN & SANDY CAREY

- Their Latin name—*leucocephalus*—means white head, which they display as an adult at age four or five.
- Adults have white tails, but immature bald eagles are dark brown with some white on their undersides, causing some to be mistaken for golden eagles.
- Female bald eagles, at 10 to 14 pounds, outweigh the 8- to 9-pound males.
- Their wings span seven feet.
- Bald eagles can migrate at speeds of 40 miles per hour, and live three decades in captivity.

Bald eagles swoop with ease to pluck a fish from the water and carry it away in their talons. They hunt rabbits, ground squirrels, and waterfowl. And they will not pass up a chance to scavenge carrion, offering the lucky passerby a close-up view of the huge hawk.

One or two dozen pairs of bald eagles live in Yellowstone year-round. They build large nests of sticks in the tops of coniferous trees near lakes and rivers. One to three eggs are laid in early spring, and eaglets fledge by mid-August. Additional bald eagles migrate through the park and are often seen along the cottonwoods beside the lower Gardner and Yellowstone rivers in winter.

Endangered by pesticides that caused thinning of their eggshells and by being shot or poisoned in the mid-twentieth century, they are now protected by the Bald Eagle Protection Act and endangered species listing. Their populations are recovering in most of the United States, including the Rocky Mountains.

A **bedraggled-looking cow moose**
emerges from among the pond lilies
where she grazes these and other riparian plants, such as willows. In winter, moose use their
long legs to move through deep snow and browse in the mature subalpine fir forests. Bull moose
may exceed 1,000 pounds in weight and sport huge, palmate antlers in the summer and fall.
Moose are powerful swimmers, sometimes seen crossing Yellowstone's largest lakes. They are
seldom seen in groups of more than four, though cows may bear twins in spring.

Beavers chew on aspens, willows, cottonwoods, and even conifers for both food and building
material. Well-known engineers of dams and lodges, in Yellowstone beavers also den in the banks of
high-flowing rivers. Beavers are slow-moving and active mostly at night. They have an excellent sense of
smell and stay close to water for their safety. On land they may be caught by wolves, or hit by a vehicle while
crossing the road. The park's most abundant colonies are remote, where the Yellowstone River enters the
lake, in the southwestern corner, and
along the Gallatin River and Highway

***C**anada geese pluck plants from marshes, wetlands, and below the surfaces of lakes and streams. Geese build nests above the waterline, and goslings are born in June. Known for their V-shaped flight patterns during migration, many stay the winter on the warm, open waters of the Madison and Firehole rivers.*

***A**n American coot tends its chicks* before they learn to fly. This gray-black bird with the white bill is not a duck, but may dive like one for submerged plant roots and even small insects and fishes. A noisy bird, especially in courtship, coots also splash around the marshy edges of ponds.

TOM MURPHY

Aquatic Areas

The park road system conveniently follows along most major rivers in Yellowstone, from the Lewis in the south to the Gardner in the north. Birds and mammals associated with these streams are influenced by the vegetation at river's edge. In summer, the Yellowstone River corridor through the Hayden Valley, where neither boating nor fishing is permitted, is an outstanding place to observe wildlife undisturbed. The park's largest lakes—Yellowstone, Shoshone, and Lewis—can be appreciated from the shore or from a boat, by those who have time and energy. Numerous other ponds and lakes, scattered near the roads and throughout the backcountry, offer plentiful and varied opportunities to enjoy the water and its associated animal life.

In winter, the Firehole and Madison rivers provide unique riparian habitat for wildlife—a result of the warm influx from thermal features that keep the rivers from freezing when other Rocky Mountain landscapes are buried in snow and ice.

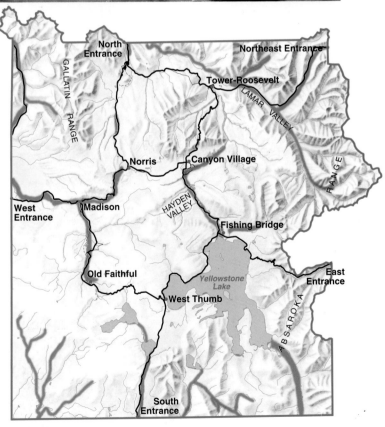

JEFF FOOTT

ART WOLFE

***S**everal dozen trumpeter swans live in the park.*
*Adults form strong pair bonds and together build large
nests during May on still waters along marshy edges
of ponds and rivers, sometimes using an old muskrat
house or beaver lodge as a base. The female (pen)
incubates and sometimes turns her average clutch of
five eggs, which hatch in June. Swans are territorial
and very sensitive to disturbance while nesting.
Coyotes hunt eggs and young birds, and human
disturbance has caused nest failure. Swans also die
from avian cholera and ingesting lead fishing sinkers.*

***H**undreds of migrant*
*trumpeter swans make a
winter stop on the ice-free
waters of the Madison River,
sometimes chasing away
intruders on their space, such
as mallard ducks.
Though cygnets eat
small aquatic insects and
crustaceans, adult
swans bob to graze on
submerged plants. Their
long, graceful necks
are twice their body
length. Listen for
the deep call for which
they were named,
especially when in flight.*

In the raging torrents of late spring runoff, a cow elk urges her young calf to cross a river by bleating and leading the way. Some of these early swimming lessons succeed; others provide a feeding opportunity for a nearby coyote or bear. Once safely across, the cow may bark a warning if a predator lurks.

Muskrats can be distinguished from the larger beaver by their rounded tails. Both animals prefer calm water and build houses of vegetation with chambers above the waterline. The muskrat's cone-shaped huts can be seen easily in autumn as water levels drop. They eat mostly cattails, rushes, pond lilies, and other aquatic plants, while on the lookout for danger from mink or foxes.

Aquatic Communities

Ospreys, or fish hawks, are often seen hovering above a lake or river ready to pounce on their prey, which they lift from the water with both feet. Dozens of ospreys nest in the tops of conifers around Yellowstone Lake, where they primarily hunt for young cutthroat trout. Here only for summer, they also reuse the same nesting spots atop spires of rock in the Grand Canyon of the Yellowstone, where they are often seen from overlooks along the Canyon Rim Drives. Because ospreys migrate to Mexico or even South America in winter, they are sensitive to conditions half a world away, prompting biologists to monitor changes in the global environment.

JEFF VANUGA

JEFF FOOTT

The continent's largest heron, the great blue, frequents the riparian zones. Herons wait poised near water's edge until a meal presents itself, then strike with their bill. The majority of their diet is fish, which they swallow whole. They also hunt frogs, dragonflies, grasshoppers, snakes, voles, ground squirrels, and other small mammals. Great blue herons often group together and build bulky stick nests in a rookery high in a stand of trees. Both males and females bring food to the nest and regurgitate it into their chicks' mouths.

Seeing a peregrine falcon, especially resting at ground level, is a rare treat. This small hunter is famed for flying speeds of 40 to 55 miles per hour. They can top 200 miles per hour when diving to kill prey, usually ducks or songbirds struck in midair. Peregrines nest in aeries on cliffs above rivers. The falcons themselves fear larger predators like golden eagles—and human falconers who might poach the endangered bird.

W. PERRY CONWAY

Summer visitors may be surprised to see American white pelicans on Yellowstone Lake and the Yellowstone River. Pelicans often work in groups, herding fish into shallow water where they are easier to catch. The birds dip, rather than dive, swallowing their prey whole. A major rookery lies on the lake's remote Molly Islands. In the 1920s, park managers and anglers voiced concern for the cutthroat trout population, which harbored parasites hosted by the pelicans. This led to a proposal to control the birds by sending rangers to stomp on pelican eggs. The plan was dropped due to public opposition. Today, the islands are closed to public access to limit disturbance of the nesting pelicans.

GERALD & BUFF CORSI

The sustained buzzing call of yellow-headed blackbirds is often hea
among tall marsh grasses and reeds. They prey upon beetles, caterpillar,
dragonflies, spiders, and snails. Males choose and defend territories
over standing water, such as ponds in the Lamar Valley along the road to
Slough Creek Campground, alert for prairie falcons on the prowl.

JOHN P. GEORGE

Red-winged blackbirds
live in habitat similar
to that used by the slightly larger
yellow-headed blackbirds. They too defend
their nests, driving off ravens, magpies,
or even hawks. A female, lacking
the bright red wing patch, feeds her
young seeds as well as caddis
flies, mayflies, and moths.

GARY LEPPART

A female bufflehead rests between
dives for aquatic flies. These sea
ducks winter farther south, but may be
seen summering along the Yellowstone
River in Hayden Valley. The male
has a large, clownish white head patch.

Both Barrow's and
common goldeneyes
(pictured) live on
lakes and rivers; the
common is seen
more frequently in winter.
They are strong fliers
and excellent divers, feeding on
small fish, insect nymphs,
and pondweeds. The goldeneye
nests in a tree cavity near
the water, perhaps using a hole
abandoned by a flicker.

TOM MURPHY

Flocks of American avocets *wade in shallows, using their curved bills to stir up water boatmen, dragonfly nymphs, beetles, and plant seeds.*

JOHN P. GEORGE

Double-crested *cormorants nest in colonies on Yellowstone Lake. While diving for trout, their large webbed feet help them swim away from predatory loons and gulls.*

The eerie laugh of a *common loon may be heard on some park lakes, where they nest in matted grasses or reeds. Loons peer, then plunge—sometimes quite deep—and may remain underwater for a full minute in pursuit of fish.*

JOHN P. GEORGE

A common merganser, here with *her young, sports a scruffy reddish crest in contrast to the green of the adult male. These fish-eaters, the largest inland ducks on the continent, have streamlined bodies to aid their swift underwater hunts. Frogs, leeches, snails, and other aquatic species fall prey to these ducks. They need a long running start to lift off the ice or water.*

Yellowstone's only native trout, the cutthroat, is an opportunist, feeding on plankton, aquatic insects like mayflies (above), algae, frogs, and fish smaller than themselves. But a large cutthroat is easy prey for at least 42 other birds and mammals—not counting humans, whose angling enthusiasm caused cutthroats to decline until regulations were changed in the 1970s. A major new threat appeared in 1994. Non-native lake trout, much larger fish-eaters (left, with smaller cutthroat), were discovered Yellowstone Lake. Unless controlled, the invaders will severely reduce the cutthroats—affecting the entire food chain.

JEFF & ALEXA HENRY

TOM MURPHY

JEFF FOOTT

Wise fly-fishers watch North American dippers (pictured with stone fly) bob along under the surface of their favorite white water, to see what insects are the hatch of the moment.

Vegetarian ephydrid flies eat cyanobacteria, simple thermophilic (heat-loving) organisms that form the colorful mats found in hot springs. The flies lay pinkish-orange eggs on the mats, hatch, and metamorphose in a two-week life cycle!

TOM MURPHY

About 400 types of aquatic insects e known in Yellowstone, but certainly more exist. ke mammals, they include grazers, scavengers, and edators. Some damselfly (pictured) nymphs ey on other insects and even the smallest trout.

TOM MURPHY

Upon a beautiful backdrop, a spider makes a meal of a fly. Far outnumbering bird and mammal species, 800 terrestrial insect species add to Yellowstone's diversity of life.

TOM MURPHY

Salmon flies, a type of stone fly, play an important role in plant decomposition. They feed on dead and dying vegetation, shredding bacteria on the surfaces of plants and leaving only skeletons of leaves floating down the streams. The flies themselves are popular early summer trout food.

ommonly called a wolf ider, this predator of ephydrid flies may, turn, become prey of a killdeer alking in the tepid thermal runoff.

JEFF FOOTT

TOM MURPHY

Spotted frogs appear abundant in the park, but worldwide declines in amphibian numbers may signal a loss of local habitat—breeding pools and springs—and ecosystem health.

In 1967, a microbiologist found a unique organism, now called Thermus aquaticus, in a Yellowstone hot spring. Life forms that live in such extreme conditions often have valuable industrial or medical applications that go far beyond park borders. Subsequent research identified and cloned an enzyme from the thermophile that made possible the process of DNA analysis, now applied to investigations of crime scenes, identification of birth defects, and innovative wildlife research in the park.

A biologist (left) carefully collects samples of bear hair, snagged on trees and wire snares near bait stations placed in Yellowstone's backcountry. Analysis of the DNA in hairs will help park managers learn how many bears frequent an area, in this case a trout spawning stream. In time, biologists hope the technique can be applied to making accurate estimates of large animal populations without the expensive and dangerous trapping, marking, and aerial tracking now required.

Grizzly bears prowl at least 60 shallow streams around Yellowstone Lake from May to July, searching for spawning cutthroats. Bears, mink, pelicans, ospreys, and most other fish-hunters cannot catch lake trout, who live in deep water and may weigh 40 pounds. Biologists ceased stocking non-native species in the 19— and never planted lake trout in Yellowstone Lake. This uninvited newcomer, possibly planted by a fisherman, may have serious consequences for the pyramid of species connected to the cutthroat trout.

Connected Strands

A western tanager, one of the park's most colorful songbirds, preys upon a most common scavenger— maggots consuming the carcass of an elk. The scavenger decomposers get little respect from wildlife watchers, but a great deal from ecologists, who equate their importance to human trash collectors performing an important behind-the-scenes service for their communities.

*T*he skeleton of an elk blends into the frost and fog along the Firehole River. Write your own tale of the elk's life and death—did a coyote or wolf happen upon it, or did winter's cold and old age exact their final toll? And which small scavengers fed without scattering the bones farther from the riverbank?

The amalgam of Yellowstone's wildlife communities is unique in its completeness. No fence encircles the park; animals move seamlessly across the borders of this wild ecosystem. Each year, 3 million human travelers come but stay for only a short time. Most barely penetrate the 2 million acres of backcountry where roads have never gone. The creatures rely on the predictability of people to stay on the same roads and, in much smaller numbers, follow the same paths through the forests and grassy meadows. Do not be fooled by animals that appear to be accustomed or "habituated" to humans. Tolerance is not tameness—wildness is in their genes, and nature still reigns in this land which is their home.

JEFF FOOTT

In a timeless scene, the Mammoth mound of travertine grows by inches, as an elk issues a bugling cry—a claim to his harem, or a challenge to other bulls?

Always watch or photograph animals *from a safe distance. If outside your vehicle, keep at least 100 yards from bears and 25 yards from other animals. Moving toward them, especially at a run, will usually only chase them away. Never whistle or make noises to attract their attention. Stay quiet and respect their space, and you and other visitors will have a better chance to enjoy the wildlife at Yellowstone.*

ERWIN & PEGGY BAUER

About Photography

Many of the images in this book, especially close-ups and pictures of predators, were of captive animals filmed in wild game farms or preserves. Good nature photographers also respect wildlife, being unobtrusive by using high-powered lenses to capture images of distant animals that exhibit natural behavior in wild settings.

SUGGESTED READING

ANDERSON, ROGER and CAROL SHIVELY ANDERSON. *Yellowstone: The Story Behind the Scenery.* Las Vegas, Nevada: KC Publications, Inc., 1998 (revised).

BROCK, THOMAS D. *Life at High Temperatures.* Yellowstone National Park, Wyoming: Yellowstone Association for Natural Science, History & Education, Inc., 1994.

DeGOLIA, JACK. *Fire, A Force of Nature: The Story Behind the Scenery.* Las Vegas, Nevada: KC Publications, Inc., 1989.

McENEANEY, TERRY. *Birds of Yellowstone.* Boulder, Colorado: Roberts Rinehart, Inc. Publishers, 1988.

PHILLIPS, MICHAEL K. and DOUGLAS W. SMITH. *The Wolves of Yellowstone.* Stillwater, Minnesota: Voyageur Press, Inc., 1996.

ROBINSON, SANDRA C. and GEORGE B. *in pictures Yellowstone: The Continuing Story.* Las Vegas, Nevada: KC Publications, Inc., 1990.

SAMPLE, MICHAEL S. *Bison: Symbol of the American West.* Helena, Montana: Falcon Press, 1987.

SCHULLERY, PAUL. *The Bears of Yellowstone.* Boulder, Colorado: Roberts Rinehart, Inc. Publishers, 1992.

STREUBEL, DONALD. *Small Mammals of the Yellowstone Ecosystem.* Boulder, Colorado: Roberts Rinehart, Inc. Publishers, 1989.

VARLEY, JOHN D. and PAUL SCHULLERY. *Yellowstone Fishes: Ecology, History, and Angling in the Park.* Mechanicsburg, Pennsylvania: Stackpole Books, 1998.

WILKINSON, TODD. *Track of the Coyote.* Minocqua, Wisconsin: NorthWord Press, Inc., 1995.

For Children:

HUBBARD, FRAN. (Illustrated by Bob Hines.) *Animal Friends of Yellowstone.* Fredricksburg, Texas: Awani Press, 1971.

The Yellowstone Association

The Yellowstone Association is a primary partner in educating visitors to Yellowstone National Park. A non-profit organization founded in 1933, the association uses proceeds from educational books and materials sold in park visitor centers to help fund projects ranging from training Yellowstone's naturalist staff and funding wildlife research to designing new visitor center exhibits and printing self-guiding trail leaflets. The association sponsors the Yellowstone Institute, which annually offers a wide variety of field courses and seminars taught by resource professionals on topics such as park plants, animals, geology, stargazing, and nature photography. For more information, contact the Yellowstone Association at P.O. Box 117, Yellowstone National Park, Wyoming 82190.

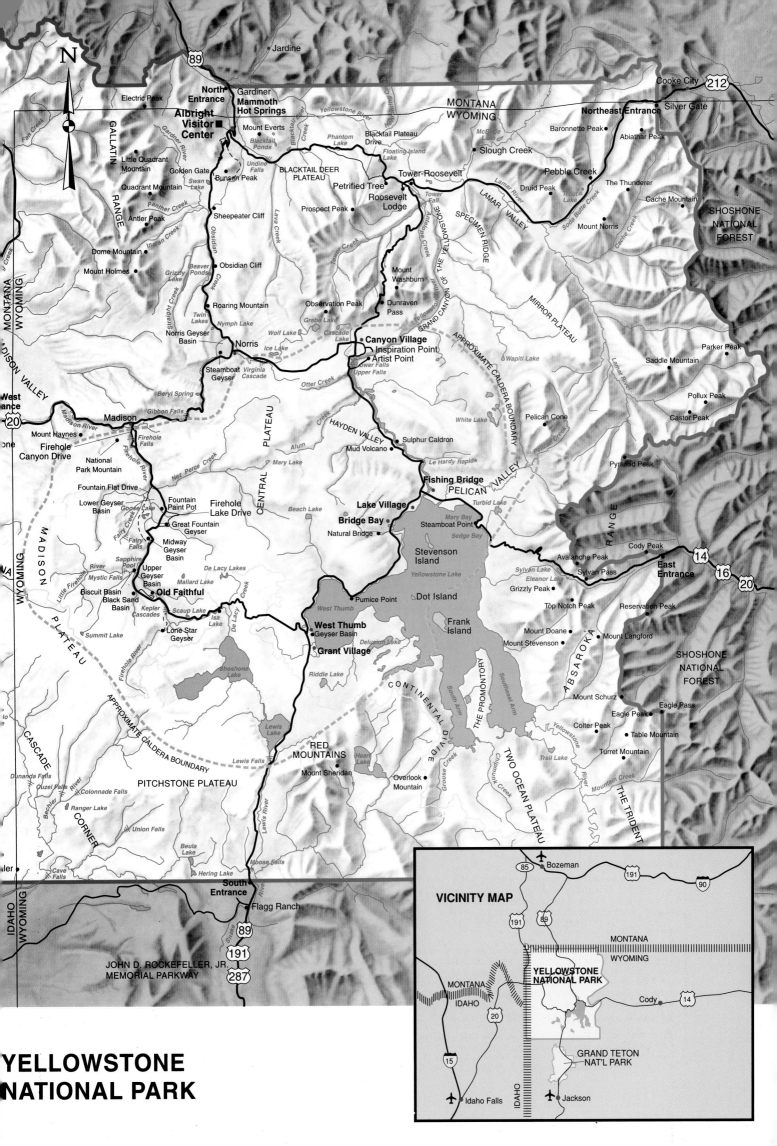

YELLOWSTONE
NATIONAL PARK

The Future of WildLife @ Yellowstone

Will the American people—the owners of Yellowstone— and citizens of the world value the park enough to ensure that the land and its native creatures endure?

National bird of the United States, a bald eagle plunges ahead to catch its next meal and continue its survival in the wilds of greater Yellowstone.

JEFF VANUGA

For more than a century, Yellowstone Natio Park has served as a model for the worl wildlife preserves. The model is not perfe people and popularity have changed it— good and ill. Yet much of Yellowstone rema remote, wild, and little disturbed by transi human travelers. To a great extent, natu processes continue to shape the untamed lai scape. Scientists, managers, local residents, a visitors have demonstrated that through th combined efforts, we can preserve plant a animal communities and recover endange species—if we wish to. Because wildlife ign boundary lines on maps, preserving them quires conservation on a broader scale than tl envisioned by park founders. Pollution a loss of habitat outside the park, from the ac cent valleys to the neotropical forests of Cent America, affect the survival of Yellowston animal inhabitants. We must maintain habi on either side of the park's unfenced borde use a light hand on the land, and keep the and waters clean—across this ecosystem a beyond. The future wildlife at Yellowsto depend on our continued commitment.

Books on National Park areas in "The Story Behind the Scenery" series are: Acadia, Alcatraz Island, Arches, Badlands, Big Bend, Biscayne, Blue Ridge Parkway, Bryce Canyon, Canyon de Chelly, Canyonlands, Cape Cod, Capitol Reef, Channel Islands, Civil War Parks, Colonial, Crater Lake, Death Valley, Denali, Devils Tower, Dinosaur, Everglades, Fort Clatsop, Gettysburg, Glacier, Glen Canyon-Lake Powell, Grand Canyon, Grand Canyon-North Rim, Grand Teton, Great Basin, Great Smoky Mountains, Haleakalā, Hawai'i Volcanoes, Independence, Jewel Cave, Joshua Tree, Lake Mead & Hoover Dam, Lassen Volcanic, Lincoln Parks, Mammoth Cave, Mesa Verde, Mount Rainier, Mount Rushmore, National Park Service, National Seashores, North Cascades, Olympic, Petrified Forest, Rainbow Bridge, Redwood, Rocky Mountain, Scotty's Castle, Sequoia & Kings Canyon, Shenandoah, Statue of Liberty, Theodore Roosevelt, Virgin Islands, Wind Cave, Yellowstone, Yosemite, Zion.

A companion series on National Park areas is the *"in pictures...The Continuing Story."* This series has **Translation Packages**, providing each title with a complete text both in English and, individually, a second language, German, French, or Japanese. Selected titles in both this series and our other books are available in up to 8 languages.

NEW! WildLife @ Yellowstone.

Additional books in "The Story Behind the Scenery" series are: Annapolis, Big Sur, California Gold Country, California Trail, Colorado Plateau, Columbia River Gorge, Fire: A Force of Nature, Grand Circle Adventure, John Wesley Powell, Kaua'i, Lake Tahoe, Las Vegas, Lewis & Clark, Monument Valley, Mormon Temple Square, Mormon Trail, Mount St. Helens, Nevada's Red Rock Canyon, Nevada's Valley of Fire, Oregon Trail, Oregon Trail Center, Pony Express, Santa Catalina, Santa Fe Trail, Sharks, Sonoran Desert, U.S. Virgin Islands, Water: A Gift of Nature, Whales & Dolphins.

To receive our catalog with over 115 titles:

Call (800-626-9673), fax (702-433-3420), write to the address below, Or visit our web site at www.kcpublications.com

Published by KC Publications, 3245 E. Patrick Ln., Suite A, Las Vegas, NV 89120.

Inside back cover: A *elk passes an day in a wildlife para* *Photo by Jeff Van*

Back cover: A *wolf issues its mou* *call to the w* *Photo by Jeff F*

Created, Designed, and Published in the Ink formulated by Daihan Ink C Color separations and printing by Doosan Corporation, Seoul, Paper produced exclusively by Hankuk Paper Mfg. C